W9-BGO-642

Laptop Lifestyle

How to _Quit Your Job_ & Make a Good Living on the Internet

Christopher King

Laptop Lifestyle

How to Quit Your Job and Make a Good Living on the Internet

Volume 1
Quick Start Guide
to Making Money Online

Christopher King

ISBN: 9780981143781

Suite 264
2 Toronto St.
Toronto, ON Canada
M5C 2B5

For more information on this series,
please visit us on the web at www.PrepareToQuit.com

Contents

Introduction

There are a lot of hyped-up "make money online" books out there. This isn't one of them.

I'm not a "guru" that makes a living telling people what to do, but never does it himself. In fact, I'm just the opposite, so know that everything mentioned here is what I've used to build my own business.

About the "guru" thing ... That title is a fluke, not because I can't hang with the best of those guys, but because I never had any intention of sharing my online money-making strategies with anybody. The only reason I'm doing so now is because of the numerous requests I've had from friends, relatives, and others who have seen my success.

"How do you make such a good living?"

I hear that a lot...especially at parties. And rather than explain each time, or spend the evening teaching everybody who asks how to do it for themselves, which is where the conversation almost always heads, I decided that writing a book for people to read would be a much more efficient (and enjoyable) use of my time.

You see, I'm what they call a "lifestyle entrepreneur." The primary goals of my business are to afford the things I want and to have the free time necessary to enjoy those things.

While I could make a ton of money letting big companies and wannabe startups hire me as a consultant or getting on the seminar circuit and selling high-priced training from the stage, I'm not interested in that. The number one reason I'm in this business isn't money, but because I want a relaxed and enjoyable life.

I want to be the guy who spends time with his wife. I want to take off during the day to see my kid play a soccer game. I want to take a couple of hours each morning to hit the gym and go for a swim afterward.

And seeing as I was getting so many requests from people to "spill the beans" on how I'm doing everything, (and that I'm not really interested in getting into the "trade your hours for dollars" business of consulting or anything else that would take me away from the great lifestyle I've created for myself and my family), I decided the easiest way for me to share my secrets was to write a book.

Actually, I ended up writing three books. This is the first one, which contains the easiest and quickest way for you to make money online. It's so easy that you can actually start today, without any specialized knowledge, other than what is mentioned here.

This book alone will allow you to make a good living online. You can stop after reading it and do just fine. However, if you want to learn more, I have some "advanced" stuff in the next couple of books (nothing you can't handle) which will make what you learn here 10 times more powerful.

Before we get started, a little about me.

I started my business in the early 1990s, while in college. I was selling "information products" (and by that I mean a plan to supercharge your stereo setup) via traditional magazines ads and direct mail. I never thought I'd do it for a living; just wanted some extra money for school.

As luck would have it, I had a friend who was studying computers and encouraged me to create a Web page and put it online. And that's when things started to happen.

Instantly, I was able to reach potential buyers for almost nothing. No more placing ads for money and waiting months for them to run.

It took me a few years to get the formula right and really have success. During that time I was just like most people – working for a living. I was a UPS guy, I was in phone sales (also known as telemarketing), and I washed dishes, just to name a few of the jobs I had.

My experience with the "working world" was another reason I wanted to share my online business secrets with people. I know what it's like to work a job you can't stand. In fact, I can think of few things as miserable.

Fortunately for you, I'm here to share my secrets of making money online. Because of this, realize that you'll be able to "shortcut" my success and do things much faster than I ever thought possible.

Why tell you my background? Why not just give you the info you need to make money? A couple of reasons.

For one, I want you to understand that I'm just like you. I wasn't some kind of computer nerd, nor was I a marketing guy. I was studying music and just happened upon this.

I also want you to understand why I'm promoting lifestyle as much as money in this series. I was the singer in a band! We didn't call it "playing" for nothing!

The band never did go anywhere, but I kept my dream of that lifestyle as I kept working on my online business. To me, that was worth more than the money. As long as I've got a nice house to live in, a nice car in the driveway, and I have enough money and time to take my wife on great vacations, I'm happy!

How far you take the "lifestyle" part is up to you. You can literally make a really good living doing this business with just a few hours per week. If you want to do more work though, that is certainly your option. I just want to give you the choice, unlike most jobs that make you work all the time.

One More Thing...

Like I mentioned, I'm a guy who is actually doing what I'm advising you to do. I'm not a professional teacher and sometimes I'm so close to the material being presented here that I'm probably not as clear at explaining everything as I could be.

Because of this, and because everybody reading this will come to the table with varying skills, there may be some topics which would be helped with further clarification. To help assist you, I've set up a Web site where you can ask questions. If you have any confusion at all, please contact me here:

www.PrepareToQuit.com

(That's "prepare to quit your job," by the way.)

Let's make that happen by getting started.

Chapter 1

Selling Other People's Stuff

The Easiest Way
to Make Money Online

Even if you're new to online marketing, you've probably heard of affiliate programs. If not, if you've been online for even an hour, you've likely seen them in action.

An affiliate program is simply a program where you get paid for referring business to a company. The biggest affiliate program, and one you've probably seem a lot, is that of Amazon.com.

Chances are, if you've seen an Amazon.com ad on a Web site, it was an affiliate ad. In other words, Amazon.com didn't pay for the ad to be displayed; they paid only a percentage for whatever was purchased via a link on that ad.

That's the simplified version. It gets a lot more complicated (and profitable) than that. Still, just to make sure we're on the same page and have a good foundation to build on, let me explain what's happening one more time, with a little more detail.

Here's how affiliate programs work:

A company or individual has a product or service they want to sell. In order to bring in as many sales as possible, they enlist the help of other people to help them sell. Those people are called affiliates.

As an affiliate, you sign up with the company or person – for free – and you're given a special link that's just for you. Then, you use your most successful methods to promote their products or services – always making sure to include your special affiliate code in your promotions.

Your goal is to have people use your link to arrive at the target site, and then take the action that makes you money. How you make that money, and how much you make, depends on the payment structure that's been set up by the company or person who's selling the product or service.

- Information products, like ebooks or software, are usually paid out per sale. The amount you get is usually a percentage of the total price of the product, and can vary widely – so choose wisely!

- The commissions paid on successful referrals to services can be paid out per referral, or per each month the referral stays with that service. These can be a great way to bring in consistent cash every month!

- If you choose to sign up for an affiliate program for links or banners, then you are usually paid CPM – which stands for cost per thousand. This means that you get paid for every thousand views, or clicks, or impressions that link or banner gets.

- There are also some affiliate programs that are called "two-tier" and "multi-tier." This means that you get a commission for the person that signs up or buys after being directed by your link; and, if that person then decides to become an affiliate as well, you get a commission for each person THEY sign up, and sometimes even further on down the line.

No matter which kind of program you choose, you can see that with some effort on your part, there can be serious money to be made from being an affiliate.

Millions of people make a very comfortable living doing it – whether full time or part time. They use affiliate programs as the foundation of their own stay-at-home business, or they do it part time or on the weekends in order to supplement their income, then ramp up to a full-time business once they're up and running.

It's a lucrative business for everyone involved – and more people are signing up every day.

However, it all depends on how you promote the products or services for which you are an affiliate. And that's where this book comes in. I want to help you create an unfair advantage among your competition and become a top-selling affiliate!

Many people who are just getting started in affiliate market-ing, even once they understand how it works, get over-whelmed with the choices out there. Because once you see how it works, you want to immediately get to the finish line and start cashing your commission checks!

But how do you decide? After all, there are literally thousands of products available on ClickBank.com, one of the top affili-ate programs, which alone handles tens of thousands of dif-ferent products.

When picking something to sell, do you go for the top-selling products? Subject matter that appeals to you, or that you're passionate about? A suite of products from the same producer? There is no one set of definitive answers to these questions. Experienced affiliates all have their own methods they use when choosing what they want to promote, and they swear by them. But, from all the experience I've had, there is really one surefire way to choose your first idea.

Once you get this one idea up and running, then you can go back and repeat the process using whichever method works for you. But, right now, you're starting from scratch.

And that's exciting! After all, perhaps for the first time in your life, you are taking a step that will eventually lead you to being your own boss, calling your own shots and creating a business where before, there was just you and your computer.

I'm telling you about this one particular method because:

1. It helps you to narrow down from all the choices you have available to you – making it less overwhelming once you start the whole process of creating your idea and promoting it.

2. When you choose your idea using this method, it will make it easier to select products to go along with it – because you won't have the additional learning curve of educating yourself on the subject matter. That way, you can easily identify if the products you choose are on the money (no pun intended!).

3. Unless you've been locked in a closet your whole life, you should be able to come up with more than one idea using this method. So once you have perfected the process of setting it up, you don't have to go back to square one; you'll already have a ready-made list of ideas to implement.

It all comes down to this moment. This is the magic moment. I'm going to ask you three questions. You answer them. When you're done with question three, you'll have your idea ready to implement.

Here goes.

Diagnostic Question #1:
What things do you know a lot about?

What are your areas of expertise? What things do you feel like you could teach someone about? Take a minute to think of 10 things you know how to do. Here's an example:

1. Cook Italian food

2. Sing

3. Train parrots

4. Find great travel deals

5. Use Twitter

6. Speak French

7. Sell stuff on eBay

8. Bowl a 200

9. Make cocktails

10. Public speaking

If you're drawing a blank here, don't worry. Instead, answer this question: Are there subjects you'd be willing to take a few weeks to learn about so you could then teach others? Think of 10 things you'd like to learn how to do.

1. Speed reading

2. Rock climbing

3. Take care of a new puppy

4. Magic tricks

5. Tailor my own pants

6. Golf

7. Write a screenplay

8. Play chess

9. Keep an herb garden

10. Increase my vocabulary

It looks to me like you've just found 20 new topics! These are going to be your ideas that you can refer back to whenever you want to start up a new product line.

Diagnostic Question #2:
Of those, which ones have affiliate programs you can promote?

Next, we need to decide which idea from question #1 has affiliate programs that you can promote and profit from. So, look at your answers. Which ones have at least five affiliate programs you can promote (at least one for each of the five lessons you'll create)?

We'll get into the lessons in a bit, when I introduce you to the process of giving free tours. But, the idea behind answering this question is that even the best topic in the world from the above list won't mean anything if you can't find affiliate programs to promote while you're talking about that topic!

So, my recommendation would be to open a Word or Excel document on your computer, and make a list of all the affiliate programs associated with your topic – along with links and descriptions – so you can refer back to them as you create your lesson plan.

If none of them have affiliate programs available, then you'll need to go back to question #1 and look for other options. It may be time to consider learning something you can teach others.

Diagnostic Question #3:
Of those, what do people actively seek?

Finally, out of your list from question #2, you want to find the most popular of your ideas, so you'll have the most potential participants. (Use the Google Keyword Tool to see how many people are searching for particular keywords.)

To use the classic example, you might love underwater basket weaving – and there might even be a few affiliate programs available about it. But, given the fact that the Internet affords you a worldwide audience, just how profitable is it going to be for you to promote underwater basket weaving affiliate programs if only a handful of people are going to be interested in participating?

Sites like ClickBank also have statistics on sales as well. And, don't forget Google! They're not just a search engine, you know. They have an entire suite of tools and services – all totally free – that let you see anything from trending topics of the moment broken down by geographic location or seasonality, to top keyword usage stats with affiliated keywords.

So, this step is really about combining the subject matter you're passionate about with the marketable aspects of that topic. Once you've done that …

Congratulations! You've just decided what your first free tour is going to be all about!

What is a free tour, exactly? Read on to find out more!

Chapter 2

How To Increase Your Commission Checks by Offering Highly Profitable "Free Tours"

I've been told many, many times that there are no new marketing "principles," only new marketing "techniques." In other words, what has always worked as far as marketing in principle will continue to work forevermore.

While the Internet is a relatively new medium used for marketing, the reasons why people buy – and the basic approach to getting them to buy – haven't changed in eons.

Offering something that people "can't resist" is a critical part of getting them to buy. This was never more apparent to me than during a recent trip to Lancaster County, PA, right smack in the middle of Amish country – a place where things haven't changed in more than 200 years for the Pennsylvania Dutch who have worked this land since the founding of our great nation.

What I want to tell you about is an interesting way that a local company in this county has combined affiliate marketing, joint ventures and lead generators in an offline strategy – and how you can use the same basic idea for creating online wealth.

It started immediately upon checking in at a quaint bed-and-breakfast. Upon completing our registration, the very nice lady asked, "Would you like to take a complimentary two-hour tour of Amish country?"

It sounded great. It was free. It was a tour. It was two hours. "Sounds perfect," I told my wife.

The free tour is arranged like this:

- You board a touring van and are taken through the Amish countryside.

- The tour guide is very helpful, pointing out the important sites, sharing interesting information and generally providing a fun-filled, educational tour.

- There are three stops along the tour for 15-minute periods; a handmade quilt store, a handmade candle store and a gift shop.

Do I need to tell you how many people on the tour bought quilts (priced at $500+ each!), candles and gifts?

It didn't take long to figure out why this company was so generous in giving away free tours. There were lots of profits to be made.

This company has mastered an age-old formula for profits:

Free Enticement + Interested Participants
+ Compelling Offer
= Profit

They've got a free enticement (the tour) and they provide it to anyone who is interested in obtaining it (people staying at the local hotels, motels, inns and bed-and-breakfasts).

Upon receiving the free enticement (the tour) the participants are placed in direct contact with the compelling offer (a genuine quilt, candle, pie, loaf of bread or any of a dozen other items handmade or baked by the Amish themselves).

That's too much to resist for most people. There's a nice quilt now hanging on my living room wall if you need proof.

The company gets a percentage of the sales generated from these three stops along the free tour. (And you thought "affiliate programs" were a new thing!)

A nice system. A profitable system. The freebie attracts prospects. The freebie converts prospects. Everyone goes home happy.

It's been working for centuries. And it continues to work right now, especially on the Internet. But, you can't just put out an offer and hope people take a bite. You have to know more than why it works to make it work yourself.

In looking at how this free tour works, having experimented with it myself and having observed other businesses try it both successfully and unsuccessfully, I can spot five keys that I believe can teach us why it works so well.

Key #1:
Provide a valuable, appealing enticement.

First things first: you have to offer some kind of "enticement" that is both valuable and appealing.

Let's look at the free tour. People travel to Lancaster County, Pennsylvania primarily for one reason: to take a tour of Amish country. The very thing they are looking for, right? People bite on enticements they're looking for in the first place.

Now, all things created equal, you'd go with a free tour instead of a paid tour, wouldn't you? A tour of Amish country that sells for $29.95 is something people are already interested in when they come to the area. The same tour offered completely free practically leaps out at visitors.

So how does that apply to you? Your own free tour needs to be something people are already interested in, something they are already looking for. Your enticement should, in some way, tap into what your online customers are already searching for.

Key #2:
Limit the number of enticements available.

The van that took us through the countryside had limited seating. It wasn't a hyped-up claim; it was the plain facts.

Only a certain number of people could fit into the van. Only a certain number of people could take the tour. Only those who acted FAST and FIRST got the free enticement. And that created demand.

If there is something that people are already looking for, and it's free, and there is a limit as to how many of them can actually get in on the enticement, you've got a tremendous selling opportunity.

Let me tell you exactly what the reservations clerk said: "We only have four openings available for tomorrow's tour, and there are about a dozen hotels here that are offering them. They'll be gone any second now. Do you want me to reserve it for you?"

How long do you think it took us to sign up for that free tour?

Key #3:
Personalize the experience by becoming a guide.

Here's where things are critical in the process.

This enticement wasn't a "free map." It was a free tour. This company didn't say, "Here's a great map. There are lots of interesting stops. We've highlighted the best route to take. And don't forget to read the history notes." Instead, they said, "Come with us. We'll take you there personally. We'll show you the sights. We'll share the history. You just enjoy the ride."

There is a big difference between a "road map" and a "tour guide." People can't resist personalized assistance, personalized training, and personalized interaction.

Think about it: What would you rather have a book on weight loss or a personal trainer? What is more appealing to you, a video teaching you to become a better golfer or lessons with a golf instructor?

One offers generalized information, the other offers something specifically designed for you. One teaches universal skills; the other offers assistance for your specific strengths and weaknesses.

Let's switch mediums and talk about the Internet. What is happening online right now is that there are a gazillion free road maps out there. They are called "newsletters," "viral ebooks," "special reports," "eCourses" and "free teleseminars," to name a few.

Most freebies are road maps. They explain, but they don't personalize. They provide general information, but can't answer specific questions.

Once a novelty, they are now springing up by the dozens every single month. What makes you different? What is your edge? Why choose you? The difference is simple: You are going to be a tour guide instead of a road map.

The problem is this: While giving away a free book or eCourse still works, it is becoming more competitive every day. When I walked into the hotel, there were dozens of brochures in a nice tourist display on the wall. What caught my attention? The one that didn't offer a road map; the one that offered a tour guide.

People don't want a map; they want someone to take them by the hand and walk them down the road. They want someone to share personal insights from their own experiences and provide specific answers to their specific questions.

That someone is going to be you.

Key #4:
Use the attention you have to educate and entertain.

When you offer a road map, people can toss you aside with all the other stacks of maps. But, when you are a tour guide, all eyes are on you.

As we made our way through the Amish country tour, we listened closely to the guide. We asked him questions. We answered his questions. We were attentive. We never stopped listening. We never got distracted. We looked when he said look. We did what he instructed us to do.

He provided wonderful history and stories that brought everything to life. He explained things clearly and humorously. He both educated and entertained us.

That's what you need to do with your free tour. Why? Because when you are the tour guide, all eyes are on you. If you do it right, then when you say, "look," they'll look. When you say, "buy," they'll buy.

And you'll rack up some nice commission checks!

Key #5:
Stop at critical points to make logical offers.

Being a tour guide alone won't get you paid. It takes a careful blend of storytelling and salesmanship. You stop at critical points during the tour. You point to a product or service that meets the need you just talked about. Tourists buy from you.

Our Amish country tour guide never came out and said, "Buy this." Instead he said, "And if you're looking for a handmade quilt, Mrs. Amish here has some of the most beautiful quilts you'll ever find. Her family has been making authentic Amish quilts for more than 200 years. And if you tell her I sent you, then she'll give you 10% off."

He didn't try to sell us a fishing pole. He wasn't pushing a year's subscription to Time magazine. He pointed to things people on the tour would be interested in. Logical offers, perfectly timed. He tells a story about a woman and quilts, and then takes us to a place where we can buy quilts.

Here's a summary of why people buy on these "tours":

- They are enticed by things they are already interested in.

- There is a legitimate limit on how many people can get in on the enticement.

- They are given personalized attention instead of generalized information.

- They are educated and entertained, which causes them to listen, look and respond.

- They buy something directly related to what they were interested in, which either completes their experience or makes it better.

With that, we're closing in on the critical part of finding your free tour for earning profits online. If you've read this far, then you understand basically how this works offline.

But unless you are planning on launching free tours in Lancaster Country, PA, you're going to need to apply the principle in an online way. That's what I want to look at now. I'm going to walk you through a scenario that shows you how to do what we've talked about thus far.

It really comes down to only seven workable steps.

- **Step 1:** The first thing you'll want to do is answer the three diagnostic questions I asked earlier and decide what theme or subject matter you want to be the focus of your free tour.

- **Step 2:** Organize your free tour into five lessons. (How many lessons you choose to share is completely up to you; I recommend at least five.)

- **Step 3:** After deciding what you want to include in the training lessons, you'll need to actually put them together. Remember to provide your participants with action steps and specific homework. Provide them with instructions on submitting the homework to you. Point them to audio or video training (if you have it) and any free resources they can use (e.g., customized ebooks).

- **Step 4:** Limit your offers with affiliate links to only logical places within the training lessons. Remember, don't offer too many. They join the free tour for training and information, not to hear sales pitches from a greedy carnie.

- **Step 5:** Upon completing your lessons, you'll want to load them to an autoresponder so your participants can receive them automatically via email when they join your free tour. I use Aweber. (See how I pointed at a logical time?)

- **Step 6:** Decide how many people you can allow for each free tour. This is going to be completely dependent upon how much personalization you offer. If you are grading homework, I wouldn't recommend any more than 10 to 15 people at a time.

- **Step 7:** Finally, it's time to begin offering your free tour. You'll want to create a short sales letter explaining what the tour consists of and how it works.

Upon loading that to your site, it's time to begin promoting the tour. First, contact your own list members. You can also visit forums and post notices about the free training. (Check the forum for posting rules before doing this; some allow it, some don't.) And of course, mention the free tour at your own Web site.

Now, the only thing that remains is for you to do it! I'm going to provide you with a quick checklist of actions steps below.

Free Tour Checklist:

Below are the basic steps you will need to take in order to organize a free tour online. Remember, you can modify this in any way you choose. It is simply a suggested plan of action. However you set up your free tour is completely up to you.

1. More personalization, less people.

One thing you might want to do is have more personalization (daily interaction, daily Q&A, etc.) and limit the number of people involved. This will obviously require a greater time investment on your part, but the conversion of "tourist" into "customer" is much higher because of the trust that is established in building a relationship with the individual participants.

2. Less personalization, more people.

The other option is to have less personalization and get more people involved. You could eliminate the personal evaluation of their "homework" and instead offer email support where you answer any questions your participants might have, without actually forcing them to send you homework to grade. Some will need more assistance; some, less.

3. Repeat the same tour over and over again.

Let's suppose you do the highly personalized version and take 15 people on each tour. Every month, you can begin the tour again with 15 new people. In a year's time, you would have given the tour to 180 people. Imagine 180 people earning you $10 per month in hosting fees. That's $1,800 per month in automated income!

4. New tour, same tourists.

If you have built really good relationships with 10 to 15 people who are actively buying from you, then you may want to consider offering related tours and continue working with participants that you have already established trust with. They are more likely to buy than newcomers who don't know you yet.

5. High conversion and high-ticket offers.

There are two kinds of affiliate programs you absolutely must look for in putting together your tour: High conversion and high ticket.

First, you want a "high-conversion" offer that a lot of people accept. This would be an offer that is usually low-cost with a high perceived value, making it something you know most people are going to buy from you and earn you a commission in the process.

Second, you want a "high-ticket" offer that costs much more

money ($200 to $1000) and would earn you a big commission if anyone decides to accept it. If you just sell one high-ticket offer per tour, you could earn an extra $1,000 to $1,500 per month.

6. Audio or video can be personal in its own right.

Use downloadable audio, video or live teleseminar calls in your training as much as possible. These add a personal touch without actually taking up your time (or taking up very little). When participants can hear see and/or you, they feel like they are working with a "real live" person, and that is important.

7. Move from free tour to paid tour.

One thing you may want to consider is to offer a paid tour instead of a free tour. While there are personalized training programs (or "coaching clubs") available online, they aren't great in number. A paid tour can allow you even more personalization, as you can give "exclusive" benefits that don't come with a free tour. And you can have the option of including bigger ticket items.

8. Move from free tour to membership site.

The next logical step would be to turn your free tour into a full-blown monthly membership site. Let's supposed you find 100 people willing to pay you $97 a month; you'd earn a whopping $9,700 per month for your "tours." (Don't assume that's too much; I know of several "coaching clubs" that have over 1,000 members paying up to $197 per month!)

9. Put together an "end of the tour" incredible package.

One thing I highly recommend you do is put together some kind of $200 to $300 package to offer at the completion of your "tour." Most will politely pass you up on it, but there will be some who will buy it without hesitation, thus earning you a nice commission. You could offer a paid tour, a monthly membership site, a package of products you purchased reprint rights to sell, a workshop or seminar, or an offline product (e.g. CD or DVD set).

Let's look at one possible free tour that could be offered online.

We start by answering the question, "What are people already looking for?" I happen to know one thing a lot of people are looking for is information on setting up their own Internet business.

So, we have people wanting to learn how to set up their own businesses. That's our target audience. We know they are out there, and they are looking.

What will we offer? Our free tour is going to be a step-by-step look at how to set up an online business. In other words, we're going to give them exactly what they are looking for, at absolutely no cost to them.

We ask them, "Would you like me to take you by the hand and show you exactly how to start your own successful Internet business? It's completely free."

Now, since this is personalized training, we have to limit the number of participants. So we tell them, it's only available to the first 10 people who respond (or however many we feel comfortable working with at the same time).

We'd start the tour off with a 30-minute orientation. (A recorded audio or video session that the participants could download would work just as well.) In this orientation, we'd explain what's going to happen during the tour:

> *"For the next five Mondays in a row, you'll receive an email from me with content that explains how to set up your own business, as well as an assignment. On Wednesday of each of these five weeks, you must submit your assignment to me for evaluation. I'll get back to you by Friday with anything you'll need to do over the weekend. On Monday, we'll start over."*

Here's what we would cover during these five lessons:

- Lesson 1: Decide how you want to make money online.

- Lesson 2: Create your business plan for making money.

- Lesson 3: Register a domain and secure a Web site host.

- Lesson 4: Create a Web site.

- Lesson 5: Begin promoting to drive traffic to your site.

Each week, you email their next lesson (which can be set up through an autoresponder to completely automate the process). They complete and submit their assignment for your evaluation. You provide personalized notes. Everyone moves on.

> • *"Wait a minute, couldn't I just set this up as an eCourse and accomplish the same thing?"*

No. While these messages do go out via autoresponder (as in an eCourse), they are much different than an eCourse – mainly because of the interaction you offer your participants.

There are many, many eCourses out there, but I haven't seen one free eCourse anywhere that allows for personalized evaluation in a one-on-one setting. That's the next level. And that's ultimately what will separate your training from every other eCourse out there.

Remember, you want to be a tour guide, not a road map. If you give someone a road map and send them on their way, you have no way of knowing if they actually will take the tour or not. They might get outside, decide it's a nice day, and go for a picnic instead.

When you offer a guided tour, they are your captive audience for the duration. It's mutually beneficial; they feel like they've gotten something great because it's free and you're giving them real value, and you get to make sure they're following along and looking at all the sites you direct them to along the way.

- *"How can I make money from this?"*

Remember the free tour of Amish country; the idea is to point the participants toward logical offers. Let's look at each of these five lessons in this free tour and see how you could profit from them just by "pointing" toward logical offers that fit the information you are sharing.

Lesson 1:
Decide how you want to make money online.

What could you do here? Think about it for a minute. How could you make money by "pointing" toward offers?

You could explain to your participants that selling information products is a great way to profit online. You could then explain that there are three prime ways to sell information products:

1. Create your own product,

2. Promote an affiliate program, or

3. Buy reprint rights.

And you could promote your favorite offers for each of those options.

- As you explain how to create your own product, you could promote one of the many courses already in existence (and selling well) on creating your own products to sell online. (Check Clickbank.com to choose a course you feel would be a good fit for your audience.)

- When you talk about affiliate programs, you could mention any of the ebooks written on the subject of affiliate marketing. (Again, check Clickbank.) If any of your participants purchased through your recommendation, you'd receive a commission..

- Another way you could profit from this part of the tour is to refer them to your favorite two-tier affiliate program. When they join they would do so through your link, making them your sub-affiliate. If they produce sales, then you get a second-tier commission.

• Regarding selling products available with reprint rights, you could mention one of the more reputable PLR Web sites that offer content for sale. You'd earn recurring monthly commissions if your participants decide to join a site to pick up new products to sell!

Wow! That's just the first lesson of this free tour. Do you see how this could turn into a nice moneymaker? You provide genuinely helpful content. You educate your participants. You clearly explain whatever process it is that you choose to teach. And you point toward logical offers.

Lesson 2:
Create your business plan for making money.

After they've decided what it is that they want to do to earn money online, they'll need to create a business plan. Basically, you're going to help them figure out their approach to doing business online.

Are they going to create a content site? A direct response site? A portal site?

Will they use pop-up windows? Autoresponders? Ezine articles?

It doesn't take a genius to figure out all the ways you could mention offers in this one, does it? You provide real help to the participants. You aren't out to just take their money; you are there to give them exactly what they are looking for. The money will come.

Lesson 3:
Register a domain and secure a Web site host.

Explain some keys to choosing the right domain name for their business site, and then point them to your favorite domain registrar (through your affiliate link, of course). Instant commission.

You can also promote your favorite hosting company through your affiliate link, and you'll have more monthly commissions coming in for as long as they continue using the site!

What really makes this work well is if the hosting company can offer added value. For example, some Web hosts offer a free month of hosting to all new customers. You could say, "I've worked out special arrangements to get you a month's free hosting here."

Again, let me emphasize: Provide quality, useful information and then point them toward logical offers of things they will need.

Free Enticement + Interested Participants
+ Compelling Offer
= Profit

Lesson 4:
Create a Web site.

Will they need a Web site template? I bet you can find an affiliate program to promote here.

Will they need software? Does your special hosting company provide tools? (Another opportunity to plug your favorite hosting company!)

You can walk them through how to edit files, and how to upload those files to their site. And you'd point toward any logical offers along the way.

Another great service you can provide here is a step-by-step guide to setting up a Wordpress blog, and how to develop it into a dynamic Web site. You can introduce them to the world of Web 2.0! And there are plenty of affiliate-friendly Wordpress packages out there you can promote in this section as well.

This is a real cash cow for you because the notion of actively participating on the Internet is still a mystery to many beginning affiliates. What person who is interested in setting up their own Internet business would not be appreciative of you detailing every step for them at no cost?

Lesson 5:
Begin promoting to drive traffic to your site.

There are dozens of different methods and places to advertise online.

- You could mention your personal favorites (with your own link, of course).

- If you offer ezine advertising yourself, here's a great way to sell your own ad space.

- You could promote article submission tools.

- You could mention the importance of building and profiting from a mailing list.

- You could talk about setting up your own affiliate program.

I think you get the idea. Mix in a few good resources that you won't necessarily earn profit from, but can really be beneficial to them.

You can also mention other "freebies" they can access to help them learn more about whatever it is you are teaching. Any of those freebies can be customized with your affiliate link. Which means, when your participants access them, if they decide to buy one of the offers inside you'd earn yet another commission – all from providing useful content complimentary to them!

Let me emphasize that what makes this work is the personalized interaction. Allow your participants to ask you questions. In fact, encourage it. The more you guide them, the more likely they'll buy one of your logical offers.

This is supposed to be specific for their needs, not generalized information that may or may not help them. It only works if there is interaction. When your "tourists" have questions, you give them answers. When they don't know what to do next, help them take the next step. Think of how powerful this can be as a selling tool.

Look at the difference between promoting an offer and leading a tour of an offer.

OPTION A:

"XYZ Hosting is the best company in the world. Click on this link to host with them."

OPTION B:

"I personally use XYZ Hosting and am very familiar with all aspects of the user control panel. I'll be glad to help you set up your site and show you how to use any of the features. I even know a few shortcuts that I'll pass on to you."

Which would you go with?

And the great thing is once you have the lessons established, it's just a matter of finding new participants for a new tour.

When that tour is finished, you move on to the next set of participants! Or, you could offer many different tours along the way. It's up to you!

Why do some affiliates sell more than others? It's not a trick question. Go ahead and think about it for a second. In fact, grab a pen and some paper and jot down a few ideas.

What are some of the reasons you came up with? Did you respond with any of these answers?

- *They have a large mailing list.*

- *They have a high-traffic Web site.*

- *They are well-known.*

- *They have a large advertising budget.*

- *They have an influential network.*

- *They have an unfair advantage.*

These are all plausible answers that explain why some affiliates sell more than others. But in each of the above listed reasons, the affiliate has a competitive edge over the average affiliate. Whether it is a large list or a high-traffic Web site, the fact remains that many top affiliates aren't competing on a level playing field.

No one can wave a magic wand and get you a large mailing list. They can't say, "Abracadabra" and create a traffic jam at your Web site. And no one is suddenly going to catapult your reputation to an exclusive "Who's Who" status.

But I can teach you how to create an advantage over other affiliates by creating an exclusive offer that is only available through you.

Offline marketers have been doing it for years – and it works great!

So, why not follow their lead and use the same techniques online?

Only a handful of people are doing it, and sales are coming in like crazy.

Suppose you are looking to purchase a new car and you visit several different dealerships. All of them have the exact same car that you are interested in purchasing. All are priced exactly the same. But one of the dealerships offers you an incentive. If you purchase the vehicle from him, he will throw in a year's supply of gasoline!

Which of the dealerships are you going to make your purchase from? Obviously, with all factors the same, you would want to make your purchase from the dealer who offered you more value for your money.

Every affiliate in a particular program offers the exact same product at the exact same price. All factors concerning the affiliate program are basically the same for every affiliate.

So, who's going to make the sale? The one who creates the advantage – the exclusive offer.

Do you want to outsell other affiliates, even though you are all promoting the exact same product at the exact same price? Do you want to create an advantage that levels the playing field with the "big boys" who have the large lists and large budgets?

Offer more! You need to create an incentive – some unique and exclusive reason why people should order through your affiliate link and not one of your competitors.

People tend to think whoever gets the word out first about a new product will make the sale. That isn't always the case. In fact, it could be just the opposite. ***Research shows that it takes, on average, seven exposures to an offer before someone actually makes a purchase.***

Most people receive the same tired "product announcement" email from a half dozen or more affiliates in a 24-hour period. If five affiliates send out the standard email that their affiliate program manager gave them as one of the "marketing materials" for the product, and one affiliate sends an email with a free, high-quality offer attached for the same product, I'm guessing they'd go with the one affiliate who did things differently.

What do you think?

The idea of "incentive marketing" not only applies to new offers, but can even work to produce sales for older products.

The best affiliate program in the world does you no good if you can't get people to buy what it is you're selling. So, it's all about making the offer too good to pass up.

At first, it might seem like you're putting more time and effort into advertising for the incentive than you are for the actual product – but so what if you are? If it gets people lining up to buy whatever it is you're selling, then more power to you!

Remember, by following the system so far, you have chosen a popular affiliate program that many people are searching for online. Where there is a demand, there is a supply – which means you're going to have a lot of competition if you've done your homework. Having a home-run incentive is the only way you're going to get people coming to you instead of the other affiliates out there.

Don't worry, you don't have to come up with the idea on your own. I'm going to provide you with some examples you can use. There are only a handful of people out there who are using this information – so you'll be getting in on the ground floor.

Put this plan into action. There are only four easy steps.

Chapter 3

Step One:

Develop an Exclusive, High-Quality, Free Incentive to Grab the Attention of Your Contacts

This is the most import part of the strategy – determining what is going to set you apart from other affiliates and give you that advantage that will help increase your sales and profits.

What is it that you want to give away? It shouldn't be just another free ebook. Come on, be original! Offer something that can't be found anywhere else.

It's got to be high quality though. Something that is useful and valuable that the customer would be likely to buy on its own merits, and would be ecstatic to receive for free by making an affiliate purchase. After all, two great products for the price of one is an offer few can resist.

Here are nine examples of incentives you can use to pull in more affiliate sales.

1. Graphic Design

Are you handy with graphic design software? Why not offer a free graphic design to anyone making a purchase through your affiliate link?

Find a PLR site that offers monthly ebooks. There are many PLR sites that are monthly membership sites providing new products each month for their members to sell and keep 100% of their earnings. Create a unique ebook cover graphic for each new monthly product. Then give them away free to anyone who joins through your affiliate link.

Or maybe you'd like to promote a Web hosting program that pays you $10 per month for every new hosting account you refer. Offer a set of Web page templates to anyone who joins through your affiliate link. Go one step further and offer a free custom graphic or Web page design for anyone who orders hosting through your reseller ID.

Maybe you want to offer a course to help people create their own ebooks to sell online. After choosing a course on ebook creation and getting your affiliate link, why not create some ebook design templates? Anyone who purchases through you gets the free set of templates in which to insert their ebook content once they have written it.

So you're thinking to yourself, "but what if I'm not a graphic designer?" Hire someone to do it for you! Visit Elance.com, hire a vendor to design a set of templates for you and in no time at all you've got an incentive that you can offer over and over again!

2. Free Advertising

Maybe you'd like to promote a product because you earn a nice commission on something you believe that sells very easily. So what do you do? Send a message to your mailing list that says:

"Talk about free advertising! If you order (the product you are promoting) through this link, I will give you four free classified ads in my upcoming newsletter."

You've created a reason for someone to purchase the product through your affiliate link instead of another affiliate's link.

You also can offer free advertising to anyone who purchases a particular product or service you are promoting. Let them promote whatever ad they choose. Unless your advertising stays booked up – most ezine publishers don't have that luxury – then it's a good use of your space. You earn a quick commission and you offer a valuable incentive to your customers. Everyone wins.

Or how about the reverse of this idea: Let's suppose that you sell top sponsor ads to your ezine for $40, but sales aren't that great for your ezine ads. In fact, you haven't sold one in months. How about this offer?

"Want a free copy of any $40 ebook online? For the next five people who order a top sponsor ad in my ezine, I'll buy you a copy of any ebook up to $40 in value. Order your ad, send me the Web site address of the ebook you want and I'll buy it in your name and send you the download details."

You buy the $40 ebook through your affiliate link at whatever Web site the customer provides you with, probably earning you a 50% commission (most ebooks offer a 50/50 split on profits). So, you still earn $20 on ad space that was just sitting there otherwise.

But, it doesn't just have to be ezine advertising. What about banner ads or guaranteed visitors? Find a program that offers guaranteed visitors and offer that as a free incentive.

Let's say you are promoting a product that earns around $35 per sale. So, you offer 10,000 guaranteed visitors to the Web site of choice to anyone who buys the product through your link. The visitor buys through your link; you collect $35. You buy the guaranteed visitors for them for $10 ($19.95 - 50% commission, since you buy them through your ClickBank affiliate link!) and you've pocketed a quick $25.

Work with some higher-priced products that pay you $100 or more in commissions per sale, and you can see how this could add up to a nice chunk of change.

3. A Service

I already mentioned graphic design in a separate category, simply because so many people have this talent (or can easily arrange for it) and it is in such demand. However, graphic design isn't the only service incentive you can offer. How about these?

- **Proofreading / Editing.** Whether it is to proofread a sales letter, an ezine article, a solo mailing or a full-length ebook, we ALL need someone to check for grammatical and typographic errors. Are you able to proofread for others? Then, why not offer that as a free service for people who order a product through your affiliate program link? Think of all the products you can promote and offer your proofreading as a free bonus incentive.

- **Review.** Do you have valuable experience in critiquing materials? Why not offer a free critique of the completed sales letter for anyone who purchases a sales copy how-to course through your link? Or offer to review someone's completed ebook if they order an ebook-creation course through your referral. You can offer advice for the first four issues of a new ezine if the publisher purchases a copy of a list-building ebook by clicking on your affiliate link. You can apply it to dozens of different product offers by reviewing things like sales letters, classified ads, solo mailings, Web pages, ebooks, reports, eCourses, newsletters, proposals, contracts, etc.

- **Setup.** One of the biggest challenges facing many people online involves setting up various accounts or sites. Either they don't have the time or they don't have the knowledge. Here's where you come in. If they order hosting, you could upload their Web page files and verify their order links. If they order an autoresponder service, you can ensure their messages are formatted properly. If they order a JavaScript, then you can insert it into their HTML code for them. The possibilities here are unlimited.

The great thing about providing a free service for someone is the fact that the only thing you are really investing is your time. This means you would be trading time for commissions earned from your special offer. Most people would gladly trade an hour of their lives for $25 to $50 in commissions earned.

Think about the potential. You make a service offer – doing something you enjoy doing anyway – and people start taking you up on it. You spend a few hours each week earning $25 to $50 per hour in commissions from the affiliate program you promoted.

It could lead to a full-time position of providing those services and skyrocketing your affiliate income. Let's say you average working 60 minutes per sale. Forty sales x $25 to $50 commission per sale = a potential of $2,000/week or a bona fide six-figure income online each year through affiliate programs, simply because you began offering a service.

Is it realistic to expect such numbers? Probably not. But let's say you earned half of that or one-quarter of that. Most people fail online, so earning $25,000 a year working from home doing something you enjoy would be a tremendous success.

What do you do well? How can you provide it as a free service? Get started.

4. Free Domain Registration

One of the largest monthly commission checks I receive comes from the hosting company that I promote. I earn $10 per month for each customer I refer, and it's enough that I am going to continue doing what I am doing to get new customers.

How do you give yourself an advantage over others promoting the same offer? You want an "ace in the hole" that gives you the upper hand.
Here's what I have done: I offered free one-year registration – if they agreed to host the domain through my affiliate link.

It cost me about $10 to register a domain – which many would say is way too much to recruit a new customer.

But, I earned $10 when the customer paid for their first month of hosting through my affiliate link. Each month that the customer continued to host with the hosting company, I continued to earn $10. That initial $10 investment was worth it!

So, what are you going to do?

Offering the same free domain registration package that I did, is still a great idea to this day. Find yourself a quality hosting company that pays a nice commission each month, preferably one with a great hosting package and no setup fees. And then get to work promoting your incentive. (Don't worry, I'll show you how to do this later.)

You'll find this particular strategy is especially effective in promoting monthly fee-based programs such as ebook clubs, hosting, autoresponders, tracking tools, etc.

Learn this truth: The majority of people are hesitant about joining additional programs or services that require ongoing fees. The conversion rate for affiliates who promote programs that are billable every month is significantly smaller than the conversion rate for one-time purchase products. The reason is because people are reluctant to make a commitment for more monthly expenditures. Their reason to be online as an entrepreneur is to earn money, not to spend money.

That's a big stumbling block to overcome. It doesn't matter how "valuable" the offer is; a lot of people just won't part with their money on an ongoing basis without some convincing.

You convince them by removing their excuse; by eliminating their risk; by offering an opportunity to test-drive the product or service you are promoting.

That's what the "cash rebate" category of incentive marketing is all about. The idea is to offer an incentive that makes it risk-free for your contacts to make a purchase. You take the risk going in, hoping it will pay off in the next month and beyond. It's the perfect incentive for people promoting any product or service that has a monthly billing cycle.

1. You get them into the program at no charge to them.

2. They get hooked and decide to stay with the program.

3. You earn income for as long as they remain active.

Here's a classic example: Aweber.com is the preferred autoresponder for most online marketers. With an Aweber membership, you receive unlimited autoresponder accounts – an unbelievable offer in itself. The affiliate program pays a recurring commission per month on two levels for every new customer you refer.

So, you offer to pay a portion of the first month's fees for anyone who joins Aweber through your affiliate link. If the customer stays for the next month, they pay and you earn your commission.

Few people quit after the first month. Why? First, because it is such an incredible system and offers so much for such a small fee. It would almost be foolish to cancel the darn thing.

Secondly, most of the members will end up joining the affiliate program and start promoting it themselves. If they refer a few members, then their own monthly fee is canceled out in commissions. Why quit something that isn't costing you anything?

Finally, and most importantly, it's too much trouble to quit. They have their autoresponder messages imported into the system. They have leads that have subscribed to their mailing lists. They have input their subscription forms on their Web pages. They have begun advertising. It would be a tremendous hassle to move all of that to some other system, and it would be insane to cancel the account and lose all of that. So, they stay, as you and I would stay.

I'd rather pay the fee each month than to go to the hassle of moving it somewhere else, even if someone was offering the entire package for half the price. Once things are in place, we simply don't like to move them. That's why people seldom change hosting companies, as well.

That means you have income pouring in month after month because of incentive marketing. You take away their risk on the front end, they love it and begin profiting from it themselves and have invested their time and energy into setting things up, and they stay with you!
There are many ideas on how you can work this idea into your affiliate marketing.

- Pay the first month's membership dues.

- Cover any setup fee costs (some hosting packages have a one-time setup fee).

- Pay for any enrollment or evaluation fees (weight loss programs).

- Cover the cost of shipping and handling (physical products).

- Pay for the reproduction charges (DVDs, CDs, manuals, etc.).

- Cover any certification tuitions (if specialized training is required to participate).

- Pay any annual renewal fees for life.

Again, the point is to make it risk-free for the potential customer. Why should they order through your affiliate link instead of someone else's? Because it's not going to cost them anything if they order through you!

There's your advantage. Remove the risk and you'll add more customers to your list – and more monthly income to your bank account.

6. Free Products

This is related to the previous one, except it works with just about any affiliate program offer, not exclusively for recurring billing programs. The idea here is to "up the ante" by adding value to an affiliate program offer.

Affiliate program success isn't up to the guy at the top; it's up to you. You are the wheels that turn the big machine. You are the fuel that keeps the motor running. You are the one in charge of your success or failure. Don't ever forget that.

The offer that the owner of the affiliate program places on the table doesn't have to be the one that arrives in front of the eyes of your potential customers. Remember, you want an advantage. You don't want your contacts to see the same thing that every other affiliate's contacts see.

You are going to be different, because you have an incentive. Same affiliate program product or service – different offer.

You see, when someone buys XYZ product through your affiliate link, they are going to get something more than just XYZ product. You will have put together an exclusive, free product that raises the value of the purchase, thereby changing the offer entirely.

Let me give you some examples to understand this concept.

Example 1

Let's suppose you are promoting a product that shows people how to create and promote their own information product. Imagine that it sells for $97 and you earn 50% commission on any sales generated, or approximately $47 per sale.

What does every person need once they complete their information product? They need a Web site to sell it on. Offer to pay for their first month of hosting (through your recommended hosting company) and you'll end up getting both the up front sale and recurring commissions as well.

You can grab a larger share of the market because you're adding value to the offer – which ultimately is going to increase your sales and profits.

Example 2

Of course, this idea works even better with high-ticket items. As an example, you can easily find extensive courses that teach people how to make money sending out e-mails to their lists. Let's say you find a course that sells for $297 and allows you to earn a whopping $100 per sale! That's a nice chunk of change – and it gives you a lot of room to work with.

Remember Aweber that we talked about earlier? Well, it's a perfect freebie incentive for anyone listening to such a course. Chances are, the listener will hear repeated references to the necessity for setting up autoresponders, eCourses, mailing lists and free reports.

Aweber is a "one-stop" shop for all of that. So, you tell them:

"Order (this product) through this link and I'll pay for a one month membership at Aweber.com, where you can put into practice everything you learn as you listen to the CDs."

Let's examine what happens here.

You shell out approximately $20 of your own money to Aweber. But, you earn approximately $100 per sale for the course, so you actually make a profit of $80 for each person that takes you up on the offer despite the fact that you paid for Aweber!

What do you think is going to happen after the membership that you paid for expires? The user is going to renew their subscription. And you are going to earn recurring commission for as long as they remain a member!

Bear in mind, these are just some examples. I'm not saying you need to use the exact affiliate programs that I mentioned above. I just want you to see some real-life application here. You can apply this theory to virtually any affiliate program you want to promote. Mix and match programs and offers and create something completely unique that is unavailable anywhere else online, and see your affiliate commissions soar.

Here's a crafty tip I want to pass on to you before I forget: Keep an eye out for affiliate program contests. Affiliate program managers always want to increase revenues, so they often set up contests to "light a fire" under their affiliates and to generate a quick boost in sales.

Some programs offer $500 or even $1,000 cash rewards for top performing affiliates. You can cash in big-time by waiting until a contest is going and then launching your special incentive offer.

Depending on your incentive, you can probably use the incentive (or at least a slight twist on the incentive) for several different affiliate programs. Keep your eyes open for contests, and you could become a top seller in several different programs!

Not only will you see the results we've already been talking about, but you'll also have a great opportunity to win the affiliate contest, which will bring in additional bonus income for you, and will usually get you mentioned in the newsletter Web page of the affiliate program as the top-selling affiliate.

More profits and more exposure – what more can you ask for?

7. Training

Are you an "expert" in any particular field? Are you very knowl-edgeable when it comes to a specific feature of a product or service you are promoting? Do you have special insight into a certain aspect of an offer you can promote?

If so, then you can use the "training" incentive as your way of grabbing more affiliate commissions. And if not, read this anyway. You might be surprised at your expertise!

Why not offer one-on-one consultation to anyone who buys a particular product or service through your affiliate link? There are several options for this kind of incentive.

- **Live chat sessions.** You can hold live training ses-sions once a week via chat room at any of a gazil-lion places online. Why not provide ongoing train-ing sessions available exclusively for those who buy through your referral? This is especially helpful for people who want to buy and sell ebooks with reprint rights. You can provide weekly strategies for building their businesses, covering different topics each week. (This would also be a great forum for recommending other affiliate programs as you mention specific needs.)

- **Instant messages.** With AIM, MSN Messenger, Yahoo! and an entire fleet of other "live" services, you can be available to answer questions for your customers on an "as-needed" basis. When you are online and can answer questions, simply turn on your IM window and they can contact you with help issues.

- **Email consultation.** Allow your customers to email you with any questions they might have, and you can answer them directly.

- **Telephone.** Some affiliates provide a telephone number for their customers to contact them anytime they have questions. These tend to be people who are promoting high-ticket items, but it could apply to any product or service.

A lot of these are support-related issues that the owner of the product or service should provide. However, nothing adds value than a customer knowing you are there for them anytime they need some guidance.

You'll find this type of incentive can add a lot of credibility to the offer and take away some of the hesitancy that many people have. Besides, you'll find the number of people who actually take advantage of your training isn't a very large per-centage.

- **Email tutorials.** Don't want to deal with people one on one? No problem. Offer some training ma-terials instead of training support as your incen-tive. You can offer a free weekly newsletter that would include ongoing answers to frequently asked questions, helpful hints and new ideas for using the product or service they ordered.

This would also give you an opportunity to set up sponsorship ads for each issue, and make additional product recommendations for more profits on the "back end."

How about a set of training tips via autoresponder? Each day or week, a new tip is automatically distributed to your affiliate customers. Again, this adds value to the offer by providing something that no other affiliate is offering. Here are some examples of how to offer this kind of incentive.

> *"When you join Aweber through this link, you'll receive the 10-lesson eCourse, 'How to Use Autoresponders To Automate Your Business and Skyrocket Your Profits In Less Than 30 Days.' Every three days, you'll automatically receive a brand new lesson that will teach you how to use the Aweber mailing system to put your business on remote control and build new profit streams."*

> *"I've put together a training series of seven 'action steps' that anyone can use in order to recruit new affiliates for any reseller program. If you order (name of the product) through my referral link below, I'll give you the training series at ZERO COST to you. This course shows you exactly how to build and profit from an affiliate program – and my bonus training lessons will show you exactly how to recruit top-producing affiliates to build an instant stream of additional income for your program."*

Do you see the idea here? You can set up your own incentive training for any affiliate program product or service. It's an unbelievable opportunity to further enhance the existing offer by adding your own bonus exclusively for your customers.

- **Digital tutorials.** You can take the same concept and simply create an ebook out of your information. Allow the customer to send you their receipt for the purchase and you immediately give them download information for the ebook. There are dozens of ideas here, including:

  - *10 Highly Effective, Tested Ways to Build Your Downline* for anyone involved in multi-level marketing

  - *12 Super Strategies To Convert Browsers Into Buyers* for anyone who buys guaranteed visitors or any kind of traffic-generating product or service

  - *The Ezine Publisher's Profit Manual: How to Sell More* to Your List for anyone who joins a list-building service or orders an ebook on building lists

Do you see how effective this can be as an incentive? And did you notice that in each of the examples above, the free ebook adds value to the purchase? Think about it: wouldn't someone who is involved in MLM want to have some additional tested ways to build their downline? That's the first thing they want to do: Recruit new members!

What about someone who brings in traffic to their Web site? Wouldn't they naturally want to know how to make the most of that traffic and sell more of their offer(s) to those visitors? Of course they would!

And anyone who is interested in building a list certainly wants to profit more from that list.

These are perfect fits for their respective products - and they are incredible incentives for getting people to buy through your affiliate link.

Many people may advise you to give away free ebooks and eCourses in order to generate leads, and "upsell" or "presell" the reader to whatever product or service you are promoting.

While this is still a very effective method of promoting your favorite affiliate program, word has gotten out! People are creating these kinds of tools at a breakneck pace. It's time to do something different!

A super-affiliate constantly adapts and adjusts existing successful strategies and implements new and improved versions. Now is the time to begin offering the incentive not in an attempt to upsell the reader to a sale, but rather as an incentive to convince them to buy the product you are promoting in the first place!

- **Audio tutorials.** Audio tutorials have a higher perceived value than ebook tutorials. So, why not record your training tips and strategies and share them in a downloadable audio file? You can grab some free software at www.download.com to get the job done.

I'd recommend that you limit your recordings to no more than 15-minute sessions. This can actually be a selling point. After all, 10 free audio tutorials *sounds* like much more than one audio tutorial – even though the information and time may be exactly the same.

If the product or service you are promoting pays a high enough commission to justify it, you could really add value to the offer by providing the audio tutorials on CD for the customer to listen to in their home or car. With duplication costs under $1 per completed CD and burners under $100, this could be an idea worth exploring. Or, you could even have the entire thing professionally duplicated at under $3 per CD.

- **Video tutorials.** Take it to the ultimate training incentive with a video tutorial. It's a fact that people learn best (and quickest) if they can see someone actually walking them through the steps. It's much easier to duplicate something if you can visualize it as opposed to reading about it or hearing it explained.

Screencam videos created with software such as Camtasia are becoming more and more popular online. This would have the ultimate incentive value to customers. *"Wow, a free 5-video tutorial set showing me how to apply these strategies from the ebook! Sign me up!"*

8. A Package

A friend of mine has worked this one to perfection. In fact, he is the TOP-SELLING affiliate in three different affiliate pro-grams! And what he does better than anyone I know is use in-centives to create affiliate sales.

Let me give you just a typical example of how he uses incen-tives to boost his sales. Let's say he wanted to promote a product we'll call the Secret Profits Mailing List System. Here is an ad that he would publish in his newsletter:

> "My good friend Tom Bickerly has just emailed me and let me know that he's made his list system – Secret Profits Mailing List System – available to the public! This is the closest thing you can get to an actual one-on-one meeting with a list-marketing expert without spending hundreds or even thou-sands on a personal consultation.
>
> And, since his offer is so crazy, I decided to make it even crazier. When you purchase his ebook by click-ing <insert affiliate link here> I'll throw in 1,000 free leads to your Web site (to help start building your list) and a free copy of my brand new ebook, 'How to Earn a Full-Time Living Online In 10 Easy Steps.'
>
> After you make your purchase, just send me your ticket number and I'll get your free bonus offers out to you immediately."

Do you see how this works? He offers a few bonus items to the mix (that don't cost him a penny because he already owns the ebook that he created, and he owns a service that provides free leads in exchange for a contest that he runs!), and immediately he has created an exclusive offer that is found nowhere else online.

Packages are a great way to offer an incentive to generate more sales. The great thing about this is that anyone can put together a tremendous package offer.

Let's say that the package you put together is a private members-only site. In other words, you set up a site that you have password protected, and the only people who can get in are the ones who order the product you are recommending.

Fill the site with ebooks, eCourses, reports and articles, offer it as a free bonus package and write a powerful sales letter that makes the person want it more than they want the product you are promoting!

Every ebook, every eCourse, every report, every article can be used to promote other offers on the back end. This member's area can be stocked full of goodies, but those goodies can be used to bring in even more profits for you!

Offer ebooks that can be customized with your affiliate information. Most affiliate programs offer these. Set up eCourses that promote other affiliate program products and services. What a back end!

You should include ONLY high-quality, useful materials in your private members-only area. Don't make a big deal out of your pitch and then have nothing but glorified sales letters. That's a no-no. You want to provide high-quality materials that members can actually use.

So, you've got this private members-only area set up. And you begin offering it for free to anyone who buys whatever product or service you are promoting as an affiliate. Now, that can be a powerful incentive if you do it right. Powerful. If you put it together with high-quality materials and write a compelling sales letter, then you should be able to see a sharp increase in affiliate commissions from your efforts.

Why? Because people would be willing to buy the members-only membership on its own merits; to get it for free by making an additional purchase is just too good to pass up. Two great things for the price of one!

SIDEBAR: Why not just put together a private members-only site and sell memberships? Mainly because (a) There are many of them out there to compete with that have thousands of dollars in high-ticket items included; (b) If you use free ebooks, reports, articles, etc. most of the authors allow you to give the materials away, but not sell them; (c) Chances are, by giving away membership to increase affiliate commissions, you'll be the only affiliate making such an offer and can generate easy sales!

Here's another great thing about this idea: You can use the private members-only site to promote dozens of offers! Think about it. Let's say you put together a members-only site focused on "Web marketing." There are hundreds of affiliate programs you could promote by giving away the memberships as an incentive! Just set up different pages for the various offers and begin driving traffic to them.

Bottom line: Would you order from someone who offered nothing but an affiliate link, or this guy who is giving you $75 in freebies for grabbing the product through his link?

You aren't the only one!

9. *An Exclusive ebook*

The idea is to put together an ebook filled with useful information – usually from a mixture of free articles and your own added comments – and offer it as an incentive for anyone buying a specified product or service through your reseller link. These kinds of ebooks are easy to put together and can actually be created in less than an hour.

Another version of this is to give away the ebook as a lead generator, offering free customization of the ebook as the incentive.

I hope you realize just how powerful and profitable this strategy can be. It's a bona fide moneymaker for those who take action. I promise you, sooner or later, your competition will. Why not beat them to it?

We've discussed nine different "kinds" or "categories" of incentives, and numerous ideas for implementing those incentives. Now, it's up to you to determine what your specific incentive is going to be.

But, you're only half done when you've put together your incentive. As we are going to talk about next, how you present your incentive is just as important as then incentive itself.

Chapter 4

Step Two:

Write a Hard-To-Refuse Sales Letter That Makes the Visitor Want Your Incentive as Much as the Product You Are Promoting

If you're like most people you're thinking, "What? I'm going to spend time writing a sales letter for something I'm giving away?"

Yep. You are going to write a sales letter for your free incentive as if it were a product you were selling instead of giving away.

Here's where most people make their big mistake with incentives – they develop a decent enough freebie, but then they blow it by putting a tiny blurb on their Web site that briefly mentions that it's available.

You don't need a blurb on a Web site to promote your incentive; you need a Web site to promote your incentive! That's right – a full page that does nothing but promote your incentive.

And it starts with a sales letter. I know, I know. It seems strange to write a sales letter for something you aren't selling. But remember, you are selling something: your affiliate program offer.

And in order to do that with your incentive offer, you must convince your visitors they need your freebie as much as they need the affiliate program product!

What I want to do in this chapter is walk you through the ingredients you need to mix into your sales letter in order to generate a lot of responses to your incentive offer. That is, after all, what we want to accomplish – to have more people take you up on your offer and order the product or service you are promoting as an affiliate.

I'm going to break down the ingredients by:

A. Providing a brief description of the ingredient and its purpose.

B. Offering a real-life example of the ingredient in action.

C. Suggesting some ways for you to implement the ingredient yourself.

Before we launch into this portion of the manual, let me set the stage about the example offer I'll be highlighting throughout each ingredient.

Let's say a successful Internet marketer named Ben was interviewed for over eight hours by a select group of aspiring Internet marketers who paid a premium price to attend a teleseminar. During the teleseminar, Ben shared everything he knows about email marketing – literally, how to earn a six-figure income every year through building and profiting from opt-in contact lists.

They recorded the entire teleseminar, had it professionally edited and duplicated, and now offer an eight-CD set you can buy as a physical product and have sent to your mailing address. The set sells for $297 including shipping and a printed transcript.

Now, here's where an incentive comes in: Ben was giving away the CD set as the incentive!

That's right. You read that correctly. Here's the offer he made:

The next 25 people who purchase my new ebook "Internet Marketing Made Easy" via <insert affiliate link> will automatically receive a 100% free copy of the entire CD set, a $297 value, for free!

That's the actual incentive offer that he developed. Now, let's take a look at each of the ingredients.

First Ingredient:
The Headline

Your headline's purpose is singular – to grab the attention of your visitor enough to compel them to read further. That's it. Nothing more, nothing less.

Your sales letter is dependent upon your headline. Your sales letter either retains the visitor, or it doesn't – and the headline determines retention.

The easiest way to accomplish this is to write a headline that piques the curiosity – something the readers will glance at and think to themselves, "I've got to find out more!" or "What in the world is this all about?"

But you don't want to do is be unbelievable. Even if you really can show me how to lose 100 pounds in three days, I'm not going to believe you. By using hype and promises that are far-fetched, you'll immediately lose credibility with your visitor. And lost credibility means lost sales.

So, for our example that we're working on – Ben's incentive – what headline did he choose? Let's take a look.

Crazy Internet Marketer Is Giving Away a $297 8-CD Email Marketing Set To The Next 25 People Who Say "Yes"

How's that for a headline? Do you see all of the pertinent information that has been supplied in this headline?

- *"Giving Away"* – Let's the visitor know from the beginning that there is something free waiting. It also helps to put the visitor at ease a bit because they think "free" instead of "how much."

- *"$297 8-CD Email Marketing Set"* – We have established the value of the freebie here, and is it a whopper! Sometimes putting a price in the headline can be risky because people tend to overestimate the value of their "free" stuff. So, if you are going to use an actual price, make it accurate. In this case, it is.

- The headline goes on to let the reader know exactly what the freebie is – an *"8-CD Email Marketing Set."*

- *"To The Next 25 People"* – "Only 25? I better read on before I miss out." That's exactly the kind of response we're looking for. You want your headline to convince the visitor to read on. And if you can create a bit of urgency, the more likely they are to respond. Limits and deadlines are great to use in headlines.

- *"Who Say 'Yes'"* – Now, we've got them reading on for sure. The visitor will almost certainly continue on into the sales letter at this point, if for no other reason than to find out what it is that they must respond to with a "yes" in order to receive the $297 CD set.

That's the basic idea of what you want to accomplish with your headline. You want the visitor to be compelled to read through your actual sales letter.

Feel free to modify the example headline in any way you want to produce your own. It's a great template for simply plugging in your own details.

How about some other examples? These touch on the various "categories" of incentives that we talked about in the last chapter.

- *100% Free "Hands-On" Newbie Web Marketing Training Available To The First 50 People Who Qualify*

- *57 No-Cost Web site Traffic Generation Tips You Can Begin Using Within Five Minutes Are Available Inside*

- *In The Next Seven Days, I'll Personally Show You How To Generate Massive Affiliate Commission Checks If You Do Just One Thing For Me*

- *Download Five Web Design Training Videos Below And Begin Building Your Own Professional Web Page, Graphics And Cover Art* (Note: This would be a great one to use if you are promoting a graphic design software program. You can teach them how to design graphics if they order the software you use in the videos through your link.)

- *Will You Let Me Pay For Your Membership? Seriously, It Won't Cost You A Dime – I'll Cover Your Costs.*

You can create a compelling "I've got to find out more" head-line for any of the incentive categories we talked about earlier, and for any possible incentive you want to offer.

Second Ingredient:
Subhead

Headlines are great, but they obviously can't convey the entire message. A subhead adds another dimension to that message – a slightly different angle that builds upon the headline itself. A subhead is usually a bit smaller than the headline, and not as bold. Its purpose is to expand upon the headline – to give just a bit more insight into it.

Here's what Ben used for his incentive:

Crazy Internet Marketer Is Giving Away a $297 8-CD Email Marketing Set To The Next 25 People Who Say "Yes"

Get your hands on a completely free set of eight CDs that others are gladly shelling out hundreds to purchase, by doing one simple thing.

Let's take a look at some important aspects of this subhead that you'll want to weave into your own incentive sales letter.

- **Involvement.** Notice the "get your hands" there? That's involvement. The headline says "to the next 25 people;" the subhead says "you're one of them." This subheadline involves the reader in the offer itself. It allows them to know that the message is not only for them, but it goes one step further to plant the early seed of, "you are going to take advantage of this offer."

- **Emphasis.** Next: "on a completely free set of eight CDs that others are gladly shelling out hundreds to purchase." What does that do? It emphasizes what the headline has already stated. It reminds the reader it's "completely free" and further establishes the offer for the CDs. It also plants another seed – "Others have paid for these CDs, but you aren't going to – you can get a copy for free."

- **Commitment.** A couple of key things are accomplished here with the closing, "by doing one simple thing." First, the commitment level is introduced. What's it going to take in order to get the eight CDs for free? "One simple thing." The pressure is taken off of the reader. This isn't going to be hard, is it? Secondly, it continues to build upon the curiosity factor of the headline. What is this "one simple thing?" Of course, to find out, they have to keep reading.

When you can combine involvement, emphasis and commitment level into your subheadline, then you can just about guarantee they'll continue to read into your sales letter. And, it's relatively easy to combine those three by just answering a question that relates to each:

1. **Involvement.** How can I let the reader know that the offer is for him or her specifically?

2. **Emphasis.** How can I restate the headline's main offer by using a different set of words?

3. **Commitment.** In the simplest of terms, what are the requirements for getting my free incentive?

Third Ingredient:
Opening Paragraph

It happens without fail. If there is one thing you can count on over and over again, it is this simple fact: the average person's curiosity will get the best of them.

One of the things that will, at a minimum, get your readers into the actual meat of your sales letter is to suck them in with a hypnotic first sentence. You just read a great example (in my opinion) of how this is done:

"It happens without fail."

In the split second it took you to read that sentence, it made you want to go on and read the next one. Why? Because you wanted to know what "happens without fail." You wanted to find out the "one thing you can count on happening over and over again." So, you kept reading.

The power of curiosity is very compelling. People want to know. It is almost hypnotic. If you can use some kind of attention-grabbing opening sentence and/or opening paragraph to make the reader think, "I've got to find out what this is all about," then you've got them glued to your sales letter for basically as long as you want. Well-written supporting paragraphs will have them reading until the very end.

Consider using these kinds of opening sentences that draw people deeper into your sales letter:

- *"I bet you would have never guessed it."*

- *"I just couldn't believe it really happened."*

- *"No one could have predicted this."*

- *"All of the experts finally agreed on something."*

- *"99% gave the wrong answer when we asked this simple question."*

- *"I shouldn't be telling you this."*

- *"You've been lied to and now the truth is coming out."*

- *"Are you <making this mistake> in your business?"*

All you need is anything at all that triggers the psychological response to find out more. No fancy words or flowery phrases. It doesn't have to rhyme. It just has to say, "You've got to read more!"

If you can master this tactic, you'll at least have readers diving a bit deeper into your sales letter. Weave in your offer after the first sentence, and you've got a winner. And then, you simply launch into the remainder of your opening paragraph with sentences that quickly describe your incentive offer as it ties in with your hypnotic first sentence.

Let's take a look at our real-life example:

Crazy Internet Marketer Is Giving Away a $297 8-CD Email Marketing Set To The Next 25 People Who Say "Yes"

Get your hands on a completely free set of eight CDs that others are gladly shelling out hundreds to purchase, by doing one simple thing.

From: Ben Turner
Friday, 3:45 P.M.
Re: CD Set Giveaway

Dear Friend:

This simply isn't going to be available for very long. In fact, there's a slight chance it may already be too late.

The offer for a free copy of Ben Turner's Email Sales Secrets Exposed 8-CD Set (Currently being sold for $297 at my main site) is limited to the first 25 people who respond to the offer below.

(Notice the personal touch of "From" and "Dear Friend" that was also added here.)

"This simply isn't going to be available for very long" continues the themes set forth in the headline and subhead, while adding more fuel to the urgency fire.

But the really good part is, ***"In fact, there's a slight chance it may already be too late."*** Bingo. They're going to continue reading for certain. "Am I too late? Have I missed this opportunity? I've got to find out."

The next paragraph quickly sets the stage for what is about to come. It also gives a Web site link to the actual CD sales letter. This is important for a couple of reasons:

- Firstly, it allows the reader to verify that the $297 price tag associated with this CD set isn't inflated. It's a real offer. No cubic zirconia here – this is a genuine diamond.

- Secondly, the URL leads the visitor to the existing sales letter that will explain the CD set in great detail. The more they are convinced and overwhelmed by the benefits of the set, the more likely they are to accept the offer awaiting them.

That's what you want to do with your incentive offer – create a hypnotic opening sentence to add some fuel to the urgency of reading and responding to the offer, and then a brief introduction to the offer.

Fourth Ingredient:
Bullet Points

The next thing you want to do – and where it really makes or breaks your offer – is to launch into a list of the incentive's benefits.

A "benefit" is simply that – some way that your incentive will help them, will be profitable to them, will make things easier for them. You've got them in your sights now, so fire away with your best shots. Give them the best stuff, the most important benefits to them.

In other words, you want to answer the age-old question: "What's in it for me?"

Make sure you focus on the BENEFITS to the reader and not the FEATURES of your product. No one cares about your grass seed; they just care about their lawn. They don't care if you have the top-selling course in the world; they just care about how it will help them. No one wants to hear about your awards and accolades; they want to know how they can:

(a) Eliminate pain, or

(b) Increase pleasure.

Here's your chance to tell them.

Never, never, NEVER try to sell your product in your ad copy. Instead, you want to sell them the END RESULT of using your product. People make purchases for two reasons and two reasons only: to eliminate pain, or to increase pleasure.

What is the end result of your product? What can they expect to achieve in using your product or service? Will they lose X pounds? Will they earn X dollars? Will they have a better-trained dog? Will they get rid of pesky weeds? Give them a reasonable expectation of what your product will do for them.

For the incentive that we are looking at as an example, Ben featured well over a dozen benefits spread out over a few bullet lists.

Crazy Internet Marketer Is Giving Away a $297 8-CD Email Marketing Set To The Next 25 People Who Say "Yes"

Get your hands on a completely free set of eight CDs that others are gladly shelling out hundreds to purchase, by doing one simple thing.

From: Ben Turner
Friday, 3:45 P.M.
Re: CD Set Giveaway

Dear Friend:

This simply isn't going to be available for very long. In fact, there's a slight chance it may already be too late.

The offer for a free copy of Ben Turner's Email Sales Secrets Exposed 8-CD Set (Currently being sold for $297 at my main site) is limited to the first 25 people who respond to the offer below.

If you aren't familiar with the set – and don't have time to visit the site – let me briefly highlight some of the information revealed in Email Sales Secrets Exposed.

- How to use email marketing to build your entire online business and pull in a six-figure income every year through your lists!

- An easy way to automatically build multiple lead lists at the same time with a one-time (easy) setup!

- How to generate much more income from a teensy-tinsy list – turn a list of under 500 into a huge profit-making machine!

- A surefire way of selling more of ANY product to your list members that you can begin using within five minutes!

- The #1 mistake most people are making with email marketing (nope, I'm not even talking about SPAM) and it is costing them THOUSANDS every month – or, how you can earn thousands more by avoiding this mistake!

- How to quickly build highly profitable lists that bring in profits around-the-clock without any additional effort from you. NOTE: Email marketing is MUCH MORE than just a newsletter.

- Dozens of profit-generating ideas you can begin using immediately after the teleseminar ends – many of which I *guarantee* you've never even thought of.

And that's just a few of the things you'll access for free in the 8-hour CD set if you say "yes" to the offer below. You'll also learn:

- An exclusive 4-part email marketing strategy for earning $100,000+ via email marketing that is ONLY taught by Ben Turner and is not available anywhere else in the world!

- Five success keys you MUST use in order to build wildly profitable lists that automatically bring in income for you and automatically continue to grow!

- How to build *tightly targeted* (a buzz phrase you'll soon learn to love!) lists of under 100 sub-scribers that can bring in thousands every month!

- How to create a viral marketing LIST (nope, not a viral marketing ebook) that spreads all over the web – bringing you in more and more subscribers wherever it goes!

- 13 "basic" list-building strategies that you can begin using immediately – many of which can be implemented in just a few minutes of easy work!

- Eight "advanced" list-building strategies to *really* turbo charge your lists, including several that can bring in THOUSANDS of new subscribers in less than two weeks!

- So many list-building ideas (that work!) you'll be shaking your head wondering "Which one of these great ideas should I use first!"

I bet you understand now why people are gladly paying out $297 for the CD set, huh? All of this and so much more await you, including:

- 16 strategies for generating income from your lists – and specific ideas for how to use them right now!

- A simple, 5-step system for earning EVER-GROWING profits every single month from your lists, and how to get them to grow on their own!

- The #1, without question, BEST way to earn INSTANT income with your lists that you absolutely cannot live without! (NOTE: If you aren't doing this, then you are definitely wasting money)

- 4 ways to combine affiliate marketing and your lists to earn large commissions that keep coming in like clockwork!

- How to actually turn your list members into active marketers of your business without even trying! NOTE: They won't even know they're doing it - but they'll love you for it in the end!

- 5 easy ways to find advertisers who'll place classi-fied ads in your newsletters, and the BEST way to make those ads EFFECTIVE so they'll advertise with you over and over again!

- A "sneaky" idea that I use (and you can too!) to pull in more profits from my lists. This one is so easy – takes just a few minutes to set up, but brings in enormous profits!

- The bottom line answer to, "How can I make money from my lists?" You'll learn *exactly* how to profit from your lists on remote control. NOTE: I bring in thousands of dollars in profits every month without ever doing a single thing (I don't even send out a mailing to earn this income!). You'll learn how to set up your own automated income system!

Remember one of the things I mentioned earlier? Your incentive should be so sought after that the visitor would be willing to pay for it. Well, here's where you make the incentive "sought after." You focus on all of the benefits to the reader. You create such a desire for your incentive that they would be willing to buy it on its own.

Higher commissions are made right here. Affiliate checks are created by these benefits. This is your battleground. It's won right here.

If your particular incentive can't be expressed in many benefits, focus on the benefits of the actual product you are promoting, and simply tie in your incentive offer. For example, if you are going to pay a person's first-month membership fees for Aweber if they join through your affiliate link, focus on the benefits of joining Aweber – and then stress how you are completely taking away their risk with your incentive. That effectively brings in benefits and further states the value of your incentive offer.

Fifth Ingredient:
Testimonials

Testimonials add credibility; they add legitimacy; they show success and they highlight satisfaction. In other words, they are powerful sales tools.

Testimonials take your incentive from "just another offer" to one with some punch. Your offer works. It helps. It changes. It empowers. Whatever it's supposed to do, it does it – and you have people lined up to prove it.

So, get those testimonials into your sales letter! If you don't have any testimonials (you really need at least three good ones), then go out and get some! All you need to do is offer your free incentive (without the obligation to purchase) to a handful of people, and ask them for a testimonial. Most will be happy to oblige.

Ben has a whole slew of testimonials for the CD set, but he decided to use only three of them for the incentive sales letter. (This continues on from the letter above.)

Hey, and don't take my word for what you'll learn from this set of eight audio CDs, look at what students who attended the teleseminar are saying.

"This teleseminar has been the most informative, compelling, thoroughly attention grabbing, and worth every penny of the admission price I have ever had the pleasure of attending. I strongly encourage this course be taken whenever the oppor-

tunity presents itself. My heartfelt thanks to you for inviting me to attend. I am forever grateful." – Greg Templeton

"For lack of a better word, all I can say is WOW! I was completely blown away. The whole seminar started out great, and just got better and better! This is truly the best investment I have made so far in my online business. Thank you very much."

– Susan Fowley

"I can't thank you enough for the information you revealed! You laid it all out there. I have implemented at least one idea from each night in the emails I sent out this week. I have already seen an increase in responses to them."

– Dennis O'Brien

Sixth Ingredient:
Call To Action

Now that the reader is convinced they need your incentive, it's time to show them how they can get it. You simply want to explain to the reader what it takes to say "yes" and accept your offer.

In other words, let them know that if they purchase whatever affiliate program, product or service you are offering, they can grab your incentive at no cost to them.

You'll want to give them your affiliate link and what to do after they order to collect the freebie. Explain how it works. Then, tell them to stop wasting time and get to it!

Here's what Ben went with. (Again, this continues on from the letter above.)

This $297 8-CD Set Is Free To
The Next 25 People Who Buy A Reprint Rights
License For Profit Pulling Offers

Here's the deal. These CDs are in-demand. They sell very well at $297. You've seen the reasons why. So, why would I give them away? First of all, I'm only allotting 25 sets for this promotional offer. Secondly, I'm only doing it to generate sales for the *"Internet Marketing Made Easy"* ebook.

I want this digital product (*"Internet Marketing Made Easy"*) into the hands of 25 people whom I know will do a good job promoting my latest creation. It is one of my best products and has many references to other product offers of mine. I want it circulated. I'm willing to sacrifice a few sets of Email Sales Secrets Exposed seminar in order to get that accomplished.

I earn money either way I do it – I just figure, "Why not make 25 people very happy in the process?"

Let me explain how this works.

- You buy the reprint rights license to sell *"Internet Marketing Made Easy"*. The reprint rights license is going to set you back $297. What it will do for you is give you a copy of the product itself, a web page to upload to your own site, and a license to sell the product yourself as an authorized distributor. You keep every penny of every sale you generate. The product sells for $47. Sell just five copies and you've made your investment back. Everything beyond that is 100% PURE PROFIT! Click <insert affiliate link> to take a look at the product license information.

- You send me your receipt. After you purchase the license, you simply email me your receipt and your shipping information at myemail@mydomain.com. I need your full name and shipping address, including postal box / street, city, state, zip and country.

- I ship you the album full of goodies. Within 24 hours (not including weekends and holidays, of course) I'll ship your album of eight CDs to you.

The entire package will arrive at your address within a few days at ZERO COST to you. That's right, I'll even cover shipping and handling charges.

- We both profit. You make money by selling *"Internet Marketing Made Easy"* at $47 a pop, AND you get thoroughly educated by listening (and learning from) the Email Sales Secrets Exposed 8-CD Set – which will help you profit even more in the long run as you discover how to earn $100,000 per year through opt-in lists!

So, there you have it. It's a simple arrangement.

It's also a limited offer. Only the next 25 people who order will be accepted for this special promotion. In fact, as I mentioned earlier, there is a possibility that these 25 have already been accepted.

If the order link below is no longer functional, then the offer is no longer available. I'm sorry, but I cannot make any exceptions to this rule. If you find that you cannot order, then please email me at missedit@mydomain.com and I'll make you a different incredible offer. But, it will not include either of the products mentioned on this web page.

So, if you want in on this one – you have to beat 25 people to the punch.

Click Here To Order Your Product Now

Remember, if the links aren't working, the offer has expired.

Any questions? Email me at questions@mydomain.com

Best regards,

Ben Turner

And with that, you have completed your sales letter for your free incentive. It's compelling. It's convincing. And now you're ready to increase your affiliate commissions!

Chapter 5

Step Three:

Create a Professionally Designed, Strategically Planned Web Site To Pull in the Profits

By this point, you're onto something. You've got your incentive ready to roll. You've got a compelling sales letter that is going to convince your visitors to take you up on your exclusive offer.

Now it's time to put on the finishing touches.

There are five things that your Web page needs (in addition to the sales letter you just completed, of course):

1. Professional, fast-loading layout.

The appearance of your Web site speaks volumes about the product or service you offer. Imagine an unshaven, shabbily dressed sales representative walking into a meeting – a half hour late – with mustard on his sales proposal. That company just lost a sale.

Unfortunately, many Web sites look like this kind of sales rep. The layout resembles either a shabbily dressed salesman, or they go overboard and look like a rep wearing a Halloween costume. The graphics load slowly. The sales letter is filled with typographical and grammatical errors, and it has no flow from one paragraph to the next.

The appearance of your Web site is critical to the success or failure of your online business.

- Have a professional layout design that is pleasing to the eyes.

- Use bulleted lists (like the one you are now reading) that make information easily available.

- Change fonts, colors or highlights to emphasize certain words and phrases in bold and italics and underline.

- Don't forget to use lots of white space.

- Use shaded backgrounds and / or bordered boxes to highlight important information, such as testimonials and research.

- Headlines should be noticeably larger and centered on your page in order to attract attention.

- If you can obtain permission from the owner of the affiliate program you are promoting, it would make a nice touch and seamless flow by using the same, similar or portions of the Web page graphics of the product or service you are promoting as an affiliate.

- Resist the temptation to get too clever with extra graphics. Instead, focus on a quick-loading page that is professionally designed with attractive graphics.

- Be typographically and grammatically accurate. Typos and grammar errors leave a bad impression with many people. It says, "If this person can't at least proofread his offer, how valuable can the offer be?" Have someone who is qualified to proofread review it for you. You want to make certain you don't send any warning signals that would discount your offer.

- As the old adage goes, "You never get a second chance to make a first impression." Make yours count. Ideally, you want a professional, fast-loading layout that is used as an extension of the offer itself. An attractive layout enhances your offer and is actually a very important part of the sales process.

The "rules" above pertain to any Web site you want to put up online. But recently there has been a trend to step away from building and uploading your own Web pages and using a ready-made host like Wordpress. Let me explain how this works in detail – and also how you can make money from including this when advising your free tour customers.

Wordpress is basically a blog hosting service. When you sign up, you choose a name for your blog, which you can then to change to your registered domain name.

Then you can pick a theme – that is, how your blog is going to look – and add things called widgets. Widgets are quick little applications that appear on either side or both sides of your main Web page body where you can put advertisements, links, special messages, graphics and a wide variety of other things that personalize your Web page.

Now, don't get nervous when I say "blog" – you're not going to be starting an online diary! Wordpress takes it all to another level and gives you static (non-blog) Web pages, sub-pages, and many more usable items that make your "blog" look, feel and function just like a Web site.

For example, let's say you had a Wordpress blog set up so that your main sales letter is on the blog's home page. You can make that sales letter a "sticky" post, so that it always appears at the top of your main page – even if you add other things later. You can go back in and edit that post at any time, if you wanted to, say, change your price, add a new graphic or include a new testimonial.

You can make your sales letter even more dynamic by linking to pages and sub-pages in your Wordpress blog, too, to make your site seem more extensive than it really is – and, again, this can be done in minutes. You can include an entire page of testimonials, perhaps with audio or video components or pictures of happy customers. With Wordpress, you can make any changes or updates you need to make all by yourself, in minutes – there's no need to get a hold of a designer or a Web master and wait for them to do the work.

You could also include a "click here for a special offer" and have it go to another page, where you talk about your bonus offers or further explain a limited-time offer you're promoting. And, you can hide these pages at any time as well as edit them on the fly.

Plus, with Wordpress you get Web site statistics built in, so you can see how people get to your site and what they do while they're there. And you can see who is linking to you, too! With this information, you can keep tweaking your site to your heart's content, until you perfect it – then simply replicate it for every other idea you have.

With your Wordpress account, you can start blogs for as many products or ideas you have and they are all available directly through your "dashboard," or Wordpress administrative page. It's a great way to organize everything once you really get up and running with this system.

There are also a ton of Wordpress packages out there available that are designed especially for affiliates.

2. Email capture form.

Another thing I consider to be a necessity for an incentive Web page is a way for you to obtain the email addresses of your visitors with an email capture form. The easiest way to do this is to set up a free report to give away at your Web page.

You'll find that many people choose to give away a free newsletter subscription instead of a report. I prefer a report to the ezine in regards to an incentive Web page because the report is designed to convert the visitor into a customer for the affiliate program you are promoting.

The purpose of your incentive Web page is to increase your affiliate commissions. Giving away a free report (or better yet, an entire eCourse) is a great way to do that. You can always promote your newsletter inside the report itself: *"If you enjoyed this report, then you'll love XYZ ezine each week with content just like this."*

You can use a pop-up window or an alert window in order to offer the report. By offering an attention-grabbing title, you'll find that many of your visitors will request the report while at your site. This does several important things for you.

- You now have a record of the visitor to your Web site, a real-life person you can contact. And more than that, they are a targeted contact; after all, they wouldn't have requested the information from you if they weren't at least somewhat interested.

It is from this group of people that you will be able to convert the greatest number of sales.

- Because you have the email address of your visitor, you can contact them in the future to follow up on the report they requested and make additional offers. This is an invaluable tool in the hands of a wise marketer. The fortune is in the list.

- The report will give you an opportunity to promote the product you are marketing, which gives you even more chances to convince the reader of the incentive that you are offering, and to convert the reader into a customer. Inside the report you'll want to provide these things:

  - A. Quality content filled with useful information that relates to the affiliate program product or service you are promoting.

  - B. Your incentive offer explained exactly as you did on your incentive Web page.

  - C. Information on joining your regular ezine (email newsletter).

3. Exit pop-up window.

Here's how most people promote affiliate programs: They promote their affiliate page, driving traffic directly to it. In doing this, they don't have an opportunity to separate themselves from other affiliates by offering an incentive; they have no way of capturing an email for future follow-up; and they have no opportunity for building trust and credibility through the distribution of a free report.

They leave everything in the hands of the affiliate program manager – which could be a good thing, but it leaves everything out of their control.

With the system that I am suggesting, they accomplish all of the goals that we've looked at and with an exit pop-up window, they ultimately get their traffic to the very Web site they wanted to promote in the first place.

Now, I ask you: which system makes more sense to you? Promoting the same old affiliate link as everyone else, or putting a bit of work into this and reaping all the benefits?

I'm going with the benefits. And I'm guessing you will too.

Set up an exit pop-up window that leads to your affiliate page for the product or service you are promoting in your incentive.

Here's how the system works.

1. Visitor arrives at your Web site.

2. They leave your Web site.

3. Upon leaving, a new browser window opens.

4. The new browser window loads your affiliate link Web page.

By doing this, you ultimately get the visitor to your affiliate Web page – even if they don't accept your offer.

NOTE: This is an "old school" technique and many browsers block pop-up windows now, but I'm putting it here because it still works. Not all browsers block pop-up windows and there is much less competition using this method than there once was, so it is absolutely worth spending a few minutes to set it up.

4. Contact information.

The final thing you'll want to include is your contact information. Whether it is simply an email address, telephone number or Facebook page, you need to give your visitors some way of contacting you. Some will have additional questions, while others will just want to verify that you are a real-life person and this offer isn't some kind of scam.

I'd even suggest that you go one further and invite people to contact you. Let them know you are accessible and ready to assist them in any way you can. You'll find this is a great way to build relationships with your contacts – and relationships breed trust, which ultimately is going to produce sales.

Going back to the Wordpress idea – (again, I cannot stress enough how easy this will make your life) – you can add a "text widget," which is basically a blank text box that appears to the side of your sales letter, where you can put all your contact information nice and visible – which will go a long way in breeding that trust.

5. Product cover.

An optional item for your incentive Web page is to have a product cover created.

You want some kind of artwork that visually represents your product. Whether it is an ebook cover, a software box, ezine picture or some other artwork, you need something that increases your perceived value simply because of its appearance.

In testing, reports with visual graphic representation have been shown to be downloaded as much as 3:1 over those without any graphics and only a text description. Why?

Because the report with a "cover" appears to be more valuable simply because of the visual representation. If someone took the time (or paid someone) to create a stunning piece of cover art for the report, then the report must be of value. You wouldn't waste time or money on creating a professional piece of art for a report that is worthless, would you?

If you're skeptical, then test it. Offer your incentive in both a text-only description and a version with the visual representation, and see which one pulls the most responses.

There are a many places online that offer cover art creation services.

And, depending on the kind of graphics you get, you can set the color scheme of your Web site to match it – so it all blends together and looks very professional.

Chapter 6

Step Four:

Get Behind the Wheel and Start Driving Traffic to Your Incentive Web Page to Boost Commissions

The only thing left to do is to start getting people to your incentive Web page. So, let's talk about it!

This book is about "incentive marketing" and not "traffic generation," so I'm not going to go in-depth into ideas for promotion. However, I do want to give you a few quick ideas for how to quickly get the word out on your new offer. What I want to do is briefly share with you my top three picks for incentive Web page traffic generation.

Here are four quick and easy ways to get people who don't know you from Adam to access your free report online.

1. Solo mailings.

A solo mailing is simply sending your advertisement all by itself out to an entire mailing list. No other ads. No articles. Nothing but your offer. This is the easiest, most effective way to see results in a very short amount of time. You can send a solo mailing out in the morning and start seeing results by that afternoon.

Solo mailings will cost you some money, but if your sales letter is put together well, they will pay for themselves over and over. A solo mailing sent out for $125.00 can produce $600 in profits within 48 hours. How? One hundred sixteen people visit, and 15 of them purchase.

2. *Pay-per-click search engines.*

In the simplest of terms, a "pay-per-click" search engine ranks your Web site based on the amount of money you bid per keyword, and then deducts that amount from your account when someone clicks on your link after it appears in a search.

You can still find bargains at some of the major pay-per-click (also known as PPC) engines and actually pay as little as a penny per click. That means 100 visitors to your Web site would only cost you one dollar!

Pay-per-click advertising is great since, like affiliate programs themselves, you only pay when something happens. If you're promoting an affiliate program that has a good sales process in place and converts a high percentage of people who visit into buying customers, making money with pay-per-click is the absolute best way to drive traffic.

Pay-per-click traffic is "scalable," which means, if you find that it works for you, you can do more of it. In other words, if you're spending $1 and making $10, you can spend $10 and make $100 just as easily.

For more information about working with pay-per-click servic-es, visit my Web site, listed at the bottom.

3. *Forums.*

A forum is a message board. You ask questions. You answer questions. You give advice. You participate in discussions. And you post a link to info about your incentive. It's all done for free.

NOTE: Blatant advertising is usually not allowed at these message boards. Make certain you read the rules of use before posting information about your incentive. It is usually best to read some of the existing posts and spend some time getting a feel for what is allowed and what isn't.

4. *Take it Offline.*

It sounds counter-intuitive, but the very best way to get people online is by going offline.

Sort of...

I say this, because there are actually a couple of ways to do this, one of which you probably consider to be online.

Confused? Let me explain...

One of the very best ways to get people to go online is through the use of traditional advertising. This includes radio and television commercials, newspaper advertising, billboards, and flyers. It can also include activities such as networking meetings, fundraising events, and charity auctions. Some of these things work better than others, but the bottom line is that anywhere there are people to be reached, you have an opportunity to encourage them to visit your online offer.

On one end of the spectrum, you could take out a billboard, get an ad on television, and talk up your offer any and every place you go. However, the approach I suggest is more subtle.

When you head out into the world each day, simply look to connect with people. Start conversations, ask questions, and listen. Don't think about what you're selling; simply make the effort to connect with people and make new friends.

If somebody happens to mention a need for what you're selling, you can offer it, but don't put money before relationships and isolate people by trying to make a dollar off everybody you meet. Remember, my suggestion for this business is to make it about lifestyle ... and part of that is having great friends to share your life with.

One of the biggest lessons I learned before my "laptop lifestyle" business took off was when I was working a job doing telemarketing. If you've ever been interrupted by a telemarketer calling during dinner, you know how most contacts for somebody in this career work. In short, they don't work.

It didn't take me long to realize that if I was going to succeed at the business of telemarketing, and actually make any sales, I'd have to establish a "relationship" with the person I was calling very quickly. Once I was able to do that, I was no longer getting rejected or seen as an interruption; I was a friend. And friends get sales!

Please, even though it may be tempting to talk about what you're doing with everybody you see, don't be that type of person. That approach is no different than a telemarketer calling and interrupting you during dinner with your family. Instead, be the friend who gets to know you and then recommends something that you'll find helpful.

Here's where it gets really exciting ...

The new few years has seen the rise of something now known as "social networking." You may not know the term, but you've probably seen the sites. Big players in this industry include sites such as Twitter and Facebook. I also include "online appliances" such as iPhones.

In short, the Internet is no longer contained to a desktop computer. People are taking the experience with them via mobile phones and things like the iPad.

People are connecting in new and exciting ways. It's not possible for you to reach out to and have conversations with hundreds (if not several thousands) of people at once.

Of course, the same basic rules apply to social media as would apply to meeting somebody on the street or in line at your local grocery store. Just because you can't see a person face to face doesn't mean he wants to be "spammed" with a link to your affiliate offer.

Like people in real life, people on social media services want to form relationships. Use what you know about forming relationships in your day-to-day life offline and you'll have good luck online.

For more information on the latest social media services, or to ask specific questions on using social media for your business, please visit me online at the site below.

Conclusion

When it comes to doing anything, "it's easy if you know how to do it." And yes, this includes making money online.

The best way to learn how to do this is by jumping in. Start with just one offer and go from there. Make just one dollar and go from there.

That is the key to building any type of business...or life. Start where you are, with what you have, and build on things from there.

There is never a perfect time to start. The "perfect" time to do anything is right now.

So what are you waiting for?

When it all comes down to it, it's not really that big of a deal to create an incentive that is going to differentiate you from your affiliate competition out there, and make you the top affiliate for all your programs. And this can be life-changing!

You've certainly got the right game plan in your hand to get the job done. Let's review what you want to do.

1. Develop your incentive.

2. Write a sales letter.

3. Build a Web page.

4. Generate traffic.

It's a great system that works like a champ. Follow the instructions included in this book, and I guarantee you will see an increase in your affiliate commissions. In fact, if you do these things, it's darn near impossible not to see significant results.

One more thing I want to mention:

Why stop here? When you complete this system **REPEAT THE PROCESS OVER AND OVER AGAIN** to generate multiple streams of Internet income. (This is where the Wordpress blog comes in handy; all your Web pages are accessible through one site, for easy updating.)

Pick out more affiliate programs to promote. Set up more incentives (or use the same one, if relevant) and start generating affiliate commissions for several different programs. Heck, you can even cross promote your offers and lead your visitors from incentive to incentive!

The point is, you don't need to do this once and quit. If it ain't broke, don't fix it. Instead, roll it out and see an entire stream of different checks start rolling in.

Good luck and please drop by my Web site to let me know how I can help you!

Volume 2 - How to Create and Sell Your Own Products

Laptop Lifestyle

How to *Quit Your Job* &
Make a Good Living
on the Internet

Christopher King

Volume 3 - Bonus Internet Marketing Techniques

Laptop
Lifestyle

How to _Quit Your Job_ &
Make a Good Living
on the Internet

Christopher King